C000058072

Patri

Peter Morgan is a writer for stage and screen. As well as receiving Oscar and BAFTA Award nominations for his screenplay for Stephen Frears' *The Queen*, Morgan won a host of international awards including Golden Globe, British Independent Film and Evening Standard British Film Awards. The award-winning and Tony-nominated play *Frost/Nixon* received critical acclaim on both sides of the Atlantic before being adapted into a multi-Academy Award-nominated film of the same name. The film garnered five Oscar nominations, including Best Screenplay. Morgan's many other film credits include the award-winning *The Last King of Scotland*, *The Damned United* and *Rush*. His extensive television credits include *The Lost Honour of Christopher Jeffries*, the critically acclaimed *The Deal* – the first part of Morgan's 'Tony Blair Trilogy' (BAFTA Award for Best Drama) – *The Special Relationship* and *Longford*. In 2013, Peter wrote the award-winning West End play *The Audience*, starring Helen Mirren. He is the creator and showrunner of *The Crown*, which debuted on Netflix in 2016. The series has won numerous awards, including two Golden Globes for Best Television Series – Drama and many Emmy Awards, including Outstanding Drama Series and Outstanding Writing for a Drama Series. The sixth, and final, season is scheduled to air in 2023.

PETER MORGAN

Patriots

ff

FABER & FABER

This revised edition first published in 2023
by Faber and Faber Limited
The Bindery, 51 Hatton Garden, London ECIN 8HN
Typeset by Agnesi Text, Hadleigh, Suffolk
Printed in England by CPI Group (UK) Ltd, Croydon CRO 4YY

Peter Morgan is hereby identified as author
of this work in accordance with Section 77 of the
Copyright, Designs and Patents Act 1988

Vladimir Vysotsky's 'The Enchanted Forest' and 'Song about a Friend'
translated by Slava Katz (http://www.kulichki.com/vv/end/sings/katz.html)

A CIP record for this book is available from the British Library

ISBN 978-0-571-38646-8

Printed and bound in the UK on FSC® certified paper in line with our continuing
commitment to ethical business practices, sustainability and the environment.
For further information see faber.co.uk/environmental-policy

9780571386468

2 4 6 8 10 9 7 5 3 1

Patriots was first performed at the Almeida Theatre, London, on 2 July 2022. The production transferred to the Noël Coward Theatre, London, on 26 May 2023. The cast, in alphabetical order, was as follows:

Assistant / Daniel Kahneman Matt Concannon
Alexander Litvinenko Josef Davies
Lawyer / Home Office Spokesman Ashley Gerlach
Teacher / Compromised Newscaster Howard Gossington
Professor Perelman Ronald Guttman
Boris Berezovsky Tom Hollander
Vladimir Putin Will Keen
Alexander Voloshin / Nurse Sean Kingsley
Alexander Korzhakov / Boris Yeltsin / FSB Boss /
   Reporter / Bodyguard Paul Kynman
Marina Litvinenko / Nina Berezovsky Stefanie Martini
Tatiana Yeltsin / Katya / Newcaster / Journalist /
   Judge / Lover Evelyn Miller
Anna Berezovsky / Newscaster / Journalist / Secretary /
   Pianist Jessica Temple
Roman Abramovich Luke Thallon
Understudies Peter Eastland, Matt McClure, Lydia Fraser

Director Rupert Goold
Set Designer Miriam Buether
Co-Costume Designers Deborah Andrews
   and Miriam Buether
Lighting Designer Jack Knowles
Sound Designer and Composer Adam Cork
Projection Design Ash J. Woodward
Casting Director Robert Sterne CDG
Voice Coach Joel Trill
Movement Director Polly Bennett
Associate Director Sophie Drake
Russia Consultant Yuri Goligorsky

Characters

Boris Berezovsky
Teacher
Anna Berezovsky, Berezovsky's Mother
Alexander Voloshin
Nina Berezovsky, Berezovsky's Wife
Waiter
Berezovsky's Assistant
Vladimir Putin
Katya
Alexander Korzhakov
Roman Abramovich
Berezovsky's Lawyer
Male Nurse
Alexander Litvinenko
Professor Perelman
Young Boris
Marina Litvinenko
FSB Boss
Berezovsky's Secretary
Tatiana Yeltsin
Compromised Newscaster
Boris Yeltsin
ORT Reporter and Newscasters
Home Office Spokesman
Daniel Kahneman
UK Journalist
Judge
Young Russian Woman
Putin's Secretary
Avi, Berezovsky's Bodyguard

Oligarchs, FSB Heavies, Russian and UK Journalists,
Security Teams and Guards

ACT ONE

SCENE ONE

A bare stage. Presently, we hear the voice of a Russian man. Speaking in his mother tongue. (We see subtitles.)

Boris (*VO*) In the West you have no idea; you think of Russia as a cold, bleak place, full of hardship and cruelty. But ask any Russian to describe what would bring tears to their eyes if denied it – and they will tell you of singing songs by Vladimir Vysotsky, picking mushrooms in the forests in summer . . . the sight of pelmenyi vendors in the streets. They will tell you of laughter in the banya with their closest friends every Saturday; the beauty of the snow on the rooftops – of eating ice-cream in the freezing cold, and of the comfort of being wrapped up against the wind in a shapka ushanka . . .

Lights come up to reveal a middle-aged teacher wearing a shapka ushanka. It's Moscow, 1955.

Teacher Mrs Berezovksy?

Boris's mother Anna appears.

I'm here to tell you that today your son successfully solved the Kaliningrad Bridge problem.

Mother What is the problem? Is it falling down?

Teacher It's a mathematical puzzle. The ancient city has seven bridges covering two landmasses: the challenge is to devise a route through the town that crossed each of the bridges only once. Today your *nine-year-old son* solved it in the positive.

Mother Is that good?

Teacher It's remarkable – and means he has outgrown his class, his school and . . . me. It means you must find him a new teacher. A proper mathematician who can challenge him, and guide him. Your son is a golden child. A little obnoxious sometimes, because he knows it, but golden. I predict he will be one of the great Russian mathematicians.

Mother (*sighs*) And I'd so hoped a doctor.

Teacher Anyone can be a doctor, Mrs Berezovsky. Only the elite can be a mathematician. It's like entering the gates of heaven.

Lighting change:

SCENE TWO

Forty years later. We're in Logovaz – the infamous oligarchs' nightclub in the centre of Moscow.
The owner, Boris Berezovsky (late forties), short, balding, vibrating with energy and impatience, is in his office doing what he always seems to be doing: five things at once.
Eating his supper, signing papers, while on one phone with a business associate, talking about a local gunfight between rival local gangsters that had broken out recently . . .

Boris What are you saying, Alexander Stalyevich? If you're making an accusation, make one.

Voloshin I'm saying your Chechens are turning Moscow into a war zone.

Boris You should be grateful. They take good care of us.

Voloshin It's not taking care of us if they shoot five members of the Solntsevo Brotherhood.

Boris The Brotherhood had started asking too many questions about what we're doing.

Voloshin Everyone's asking, Boris, everyone. And we could get away with it when it was a few cars. Buying low, selling high. But this latest deal. Thirty-five thousand cars.

Boris That's just the first consignment. You're going to be a rich man.

Voloshin No good being rich if I'm dead.

Boris It's always good being rich.

Rrring: a second telephone rings.

Just a second . . .

Boris answers.

Is this a quick one or a long one?

Wife It's Elizabetha.

A waiter enters with a plate of food.

Boris I haven't got the time now to discuss Elizabetha.

Wife She's your daughter. She's in a state.

Boris She's seventeen and female. Of course she's in a state. That combination alone makes her clinically insane.

Boris tries the food. Promptly chokes.

Wife She needs to talk to you.

Boris All right. One second. (*To waiter.*) I can't eat this. Red snapper? Fucking Armenian. What do Armenians know about red snapper? Tell him to make me an omelette. (*To wife.*) Nina, stay there. I was just in the middle of something.

Click: Boris switches back to his business associate . . .

Look, I was only trying to do you a favour by involving you. You want me to buy out your share?

Voloshin I do. I want a quiet life.

Boris This country has been quiet for fifty years. Not just quiet. In a coma. Now it's finally awake, infinity is at play and all you want is a quiet life? Fine, I'll buy out your share. I'll transfer a million dollars tomorrow morning.

Voloshin A million?

Boris Or two million in a year's time. You choose.

Voloshin I'll take the million tomorrow.

Boris I did my PhD in decision-making theory. I understand more about decisions than anyone, and *that*, my friend, is a bad decision.

Voloshin Being alive with a million dollars in my pocket feels like a good decision to *me*. Being rid of Boris Berezovsky feels like a good decision, too. And you can keep your speeches about infinity. Infinity is what you experience when you're dead.

Click: Voloshin hangs up. Boris hangs up. An assistant appears in the doorway.

Boris What is it? I have to speak to my daughter.

Assistant The Deputy Mayor of St Petersburg? Want me to get rid of him?

Boris The Deputy . . . who? (*Remembering.*) Oh, no . . . put him through. But will you speak to Elizabetha?

Assistant Your daughter? What do I say?

Boris Nothing. Just listen. That's all she wants. Someone to listen to her. (*Picking up phone.*) Remind me? Name?

Assistant (*checking notes*) Putin. Vladimir.

4

Click: Boris switches calls . . .

Boris Deputy Mayor Putin, so very kind of you to make time. My name is Berezovsky. You don't know me.

Putin Respected Mr Berezovsky, one would have to live on another planet not to know you!

Boris My company, which, among other things, sells automobiles, would like to set up a dealership in the centre of your great Hero City. And would like your support.

Putin It would be a pleasure to hear your plans, but I should mention there is a process for this, and a department at the Town Hall, with applications.

Boris Deputy Mayor, may I speak frankly? I'm not good with 'Town Halls' and 'applications'. So many little people getting in the way, with names one forgets. In the end it will land on your desk anyway, so I was hoping we could cut to the quick. Decision-maker to decision-maker. (*Flattering.*) Equal to equal.

Putin Where do you want it?

Boris In the Nevsky.

Putin Everyone wants to be in the Nevsky Prospekt in St Petersburg. There is a long waiting line.

Boris I'm sure, but I'm as bad with 'waiting lines' as I am with 'Town Halls' and 'applications'. And was wondering precisely what it would take to jump that line . . .

Rrring: Boris's mobile phone starts.

No, no, not now!!

Boris hisses at his assistant . . .

Here!! Fuck. *Fuck!* Take it! Take it!!

The assistant takes it. Checks the screen.

Assistant Are you sure? It's her!

Boris Who?

Assistant (*with significance*) Her!!

Boris Really? She calls me now?

Click: switches to Putin.

Deputy Mayor . . . excuse me for just one moment.

Click: switches back again. At the other end is a girl of inappropriate age, Katya.

(*Instantly charming.*) You remembered the password?

Katya 'Aristotle'. It was like magic. They put me straight through.

Boris Katya darling, I'm so happy to hear from you, really, over the moon, but I cannot talk now. May I call you back?

Katya No. I'm in a shop. In St Moritz. And it's my birthday.

Boris Many happy returns, my darling!

Katya Would you like to know how old I am today?

Boris Is it important? I always say, age is just a number.

Katya But as a mathematician you also said that numbers are the only thing we can truly trust.

Boris Did I say that?

Katya You also said you wanted to buy me something special one day. Well, I've found something veeery special, and the people in the shop said if I paid today they might give me a discount.

Boris *Did* they?

Katya They *did*!

Boris That's wonderful. But, darling, I really *am* in the middle of something. Can we discuss it when I see you? When *will* I see you?

Katya I guess that all depends.

Boris Be reassured, I will shortly give this telephone to my assistant who will be happy to arrange payment for this veeery special something.

Katya Thank you, darling. And when you discover what the number was that I spent today, I urge you to consider the number it could have been if I'd come with a lawyer.

Katya hangs up. Click: Boris hangs up, thrown. Then switches call.

Boris Deputy Mayor, forgive me. Where were we?

Putin I was about to make clear that I don't accept bribes.

Boris I wasn't talking about bribes. Just incentives. What car do you drive?

Putin A Zaporozhets.

Boris Are you mad? An important man like you can't be seen in a piece of shit like that.

Putin It has sentimental value. It used to belong to my parents.

Boris Oh, I'm so sorry.

Putin My father was a handyman, invalided in the war. A hero. And my mother, after she lost her first two sons, cleaned other people's houses.

Boris And this is the car they worked for. And toiled for. Good honest Soviets. Who never enjoyed any comforts or privileges. And as their son you remember the looks on their faces, the pride, as they took delivery of it the first time, and you want to honour that, I understand. *But*, have you seen the new Lada?

Putin Yes.

Boris And?

Putin It's a beautiful car.

Boris Have you seen the new Mercedes?

Putin Of course. In magazines.

Boris Volodya, you're married?

Putin Yes.

Boris What is your wife's name?

Putin Lyudmila.

Boris You have children?

Putin Two daughters.

Boris How charming. Wouldn't it make these three women proud to see their husband and father, their king, their pasha, the Deputy Mayor of St Petersburg, driving a . . . Mercedes?

Putin Yes. And one day, perhaps, when I have earned enough money . . .

Boris That day could be today.

Putin Really, I must refuse.

Boris I'll throw in tinted windows.

Putin I'm sorry.

Boris Upgraded stereo.

Putin Like I said . . .

Boris An extra set of winter tyres?

Putin Really, I don't take bribes.

Boris 'Don't take bribes'? C'mon, are you even Russian? That's like saying you don't jerk off.

At that moment, Boris's assistant comes in, holding a phone as if it is scorching hot, urgently indicating the landline.

Assistant Korzhakov!!

Boris The man himself, or some flunky?

Assistant Oh, no. It's Korzhakov.

The reaction on Boris's face is instant:

Boris Deputy Mayor, excuse me, I must go. I have the Head of the Presidential Security Services waiting.

Click: he dumps Putin. Boris hesitates, summoning courage (this won't be easy), and picks up . . .

Thank you for calling me back.

Korzhakov Doing so makes me sick. If I had my way, I wouldn't talk to you at all. You and your kind.

Boris Businessmen?

Korzhakov And other words.

Boris Jews?

Korzhakov I didn't say that.

Boris But you thought it, Alexander Vasilyevich.

Korzhakov Well, I could not help noticing that there are too many Berezovskys, Gusinskys, Khodorkovskys, Avens and Fridmans, like a swarm of bees around our President with slippery ideas for banks, shares, dividends and other capitalist mirages. Befuddling him. Hypnotising him. Tempting him with riches. You oligarchs are alien to our Russian soul. You sing siren songs for liberal economies and democracy, but what kind of democracy is it when seven bankers hold the President by the balls?

Boris Precisely the kind of a democracy created eight hundred years ago in Britain when a group of wealthy noblemen came up with the idea of Magna Carta while, as you say, holding the monarch by the balls. We are the instigators of the Russian Magna Carta.

Korzhakov I know my history. Those Barons were called 'Robber Barons'. And you are the 'Robber Jews' ruining this Federation.

Boris Businessmen saving it.

Korzhakov Thieves plundering it. Raping it.

Boris What is it? Why are so many 'principled' old socialists such hateful anti-Semites?

Korzhakov Listen, you little cunt, the only reason I'm talking to you now, the only reason anyone at the Kremlin is willing to give you the time of day, as opposed to throwing you in jail, is because President Yeltsin is so cuckoo about his daughter, and she is so cuckoo about that long-haired hippie-dippie succubus whose piece of shit book . . .

Boris Whose esteemed presidential biography . . .

Korzhakov . . . *you* published. So now you're 'everyone's new best fucking friend'.

Boris Exactly the title you used to have. I remember when I first heard that a bodyguard had inveigled his way into the inner circle.

Korzhakov People like to feel secure.

Boris Trust me, feeling rich is better. And feeling powerful even better than that, and that's precisely what I will make our President. Rich, powerful and secure in his job if I'm permitted to buy a controlling stake in the State television channel, ORT.

Korzhakov What do you even know about television?

Boris I know that it manages opinion. And Yeltsin cannot be seen to control it, but if I were to control it, I could look after his interests. And keep him in power, which is in *all* our interests.

The assistant comes in –

Assistant The kid is here.

Boris (*volcanic*) NOT NOW! DON'T COME TO ME NOW WITH THE FUCKING KID!!

Boris goes back to Korzhakov, all smiles.

Is that a yes?

Korzhakov (*reluctant*) I'll speak to his daughter.

Boris Thank you, Alexander Vasilyevich! You won't regret it!

Boris hangs up, triumphant.

Tell the driver to start the car and tell the lawyers to draft a contract. I'll be at their offices in twenty minutes to sign. And make sure there are entertaining people here tonight. We are going to celebrate.

Assistant And the kid?

Boris What about 'the kid'?

Assistant Two months he's been waiting for this meeting! I've cancelled him so many times. He's right here . . .

Boris Fuck the fucking kid. I'm busy.

Boris walks out of the (back) door, phones still ringing in his pockets. The assistant goes but is blocked in the doorway by . . . A tall, young man – mid-twenties, who we sense has overheard all this – now enters: 'The Kid'.

Assistant Sorry. I tried.

A young, bearded, gangly Roman Abramovich.

Roman This his office?

Assistant Yes.

Roman May I?

Assistant (*'weird'*) Sure.

Roman enters. He looks around, as if in a shrine. He looks at the desk. Indicates the chair. Roman sits carefully in the chair. Swivels like Berezovsky had done. An almost religious experience. Gets to his feet.

Roman You'll find us another time? It will be worth his while. I promise.

Roman takes a last look at the office. Then turns. They are about to walk out, when, suddenly . . . BOOOM! The building is rocked by a huge explosion. Blackout. Over this: the sound of Russian television news.

Television (*in Russian*) A huge car bomb rocked Central Moscow today as an attempt was made on the life of Boris Berezovsky – the latest in a string of high-profile attacks and assassinations in the capital as Russia descends into apparent lawlessness. In this violent world, controversial businessman Boris Berezovsky looms like a giant shadow. In a recent interview he said, 'Russia is undergoing a second revolution, but unlike 1917 this one will have a happy outcome,' but it seems not everyone is happy.

*A hospital bedroom. A badly burned, and heavily
bandaged Boris is in bed attached to monitors watching
a television, which plays news. It's reporting the attack
on Boris. A visitor enters. Boris's bespectacled lawyer.*

Lawyer It's a miracle. Thank God you're alive. You heard
about the driver?

Boris Mikhail? His head landed on my lap. Like a
watermelon. (*A beat.*) Tell me you made it to ORT?

Lawyer I did.

Boris And you have the contract?

Lawyer I do. Just needs your signature.

*The lawyer produces a contract. Boris signs with
difficulty. In pain.*

Congratulations. The number one television station in
Russia is effectively yours.

Boris Then as the first order of business you can tell them
to start using more flattering photographs of their new
proprietor. (*Indicating TV.*) Those images make me look
like Rumpelstiltskin.

Lawyer Yes, boss.

Boris Second order of business is to get me out of here.
The nurses are unspeakably ugly and *male*.

A lumpen (male) nurse comes in.

Nurse Some policemen here to see you. And we need you
to piss in this.

He passes Boris a bedpan. Then goes.

Boris (*pulls face/indicates*) See what I mean? Some potato-faced conscript from a labour camp in the Urals. I will recover far quicker at home with beautiful Muscovite nurses.

Several athletic, fit men enter. A State Security Service team come to investigate the car explosion.

Litvinenko Berezovsky, Boris?

Boris Who's asking? I don't believe we've had the pleasure.

Litvinenko Lieutenant-Colonel Litvinenko. (*Shows ID.*) Anti-Organised-Crime Unit. You, sir, are a lucky man. You have any recollection of what happened?

Boris I remember coming out of my offices and walking to my car . . .

Litvinenko Your Mercedes?

Boris Ye-es.

Litvinenko Your S-Class Mercedes?

Boris Ye-es. And instructing the driver to go to my lawyer's offices.

Litvinenko Is it as nice as they say?

Boris (*'weird'*) It's a car.

Litvinenko It's a Mercedes. List price, what? Ballpark?

Boris (*'weird'*) Do I look like a man who pays list price? Anyway we reached the car. I remember getting in. And then . . . (*Gestures: BOOM.*)

Litvinenko Did you happen to notice a small grey Opel parked by your S-Class Mercedes?

Boris No.

Litvinenko It was filled with explosives and detonated to blow up as you passed. You have, if you don't mind me saying, a security problem.

Boris In which sense?

Litvinenko The people looking after you are not up to the job.

Boris Particularly not now that they are dead.

Litvinenko First-class professionals would never have made these mistakes.

Boris And where might I find first-class professionals to replace them?

Litvinenko Well, there's one in this room right now. An elite Russian Army officer with front-line combat and anti-terror experience.

Boris Then come and work for me.

Litvinenko No, thanks.

Boris Why not? I might be a *very* generous employer.

Litvinenko I've already got a job. The only job I've ever wanted.

Boris What does being Lieutenant-Colonel of the FSB pay? If you don't mind me asking.

Litvinenko It pays satisfaction. And pride. And honour.

Boris And Rubles?

Litvinenko Three million.

Boris A month?

Litvinenko (*'asshole'*) A year.

A silence. Boris can hardly comprehend such tiny sums.

Boris What if I were to double it? Make you Head of my Personal Security?

Litvinenko Thanks, but no, thanks.

Boris Why? Work with me here. Are you married?

Litvinenko Yes. My wife's a teacher.

Boris Of what? Please say mathematics.

Litvinenko Ballroom dancing.

Boris Children?

Litvinenko Two. A third on the way.

Boris In bygone days, I could understand someone dreaming of a career in the FSB. The security services were like aristocrats, they ran the entire Soviet Union. But now? It's a cesspit . . . full of bitter old Chekists angry that the world is changing. Come work for me.

Litvinenko I work for my country.

Boris I work for our country, too. As a matter of fact, I am trying to save it.

Litvinenko No, thanks.

Boris I will double your income.

Litvinenko No, thanks.

Boris All right. I'll treble it.

Litvinenko No, thanks.

Litvinenko ges. Boris is left staring.

Boris WHY WILL NO ONE TAKE MY FUCKING MONEY?

*1960. Young Boris is brought to the modest apartment
of a renowned Russian mathematician for additional,
advanced tuition.*

Mother Professor Perelman?

Perelman Mrs Berezovsky. And you . . . must be young
Boris.

They shake hands.

Mother We have come today because we have been led
to believe that in certain cases, *exceptional* cases, you
put your own work as a mathematician to one side,
and provide tuition for people of remarkable ability.

Perelman In a career spanning forty years I have done
so only twice and regretted it on both occasions. I have
neither the patience to be a teacher nor the tolerance to
engage with inferior minds.

Mother He might infuriate you. I don't think he will
disappoint you. We have come a long way. At least speak
to him?

Perelman All right. Two minutes. Leave us.

He shows her out. He and Boris are left alone.

Boris Mothers.

Perelman Yes. I still live with mine.

Boris Oh. (*'Weirdo'.*) Why not a wife?

Perelman Having a wife would involve finding one first
and since I am interested only in pure mathematics, not in
making a woman happy, the deprivation and loneliness she
would ultimately feel would only make us both wretched.
A mother is more efficient than a wife – since you don't

have to waste time earning her devotion. The love is already a given. And unlike a wife, feeding me, washing my clothes and leaving me to my work actually makes her happy. (*A beat.*) Does this seem reasonable?

Boris Entirely.

A beat. Then:

Perelman What is it that you want to achieve with mathematics, Boris?

Boris To win the Nobel Prize.

Perelman If you wanted to make an impression on me, that was an unfortunate start. Apart from being infantile and narcissistic, it's too vain in its desires. It's not pure.

Boris Of course it's pure. It's pure ambition. Ambition is the belief that the infinite is possible.

Perelman The infinite is certainly possible. As mathematicians we know that.

Boris Only on paper. With pen. And in here.

Perelman I can think of no better places to experience the infinite.

Boris And I can think of nothing better than the Nobel Prize. They pay a million dollars.

Perelman What would you do with a million dollars?

Boris Gloat.

Perelman And how do you propose to win this million?

Boris By establishing a cognitive basis for common human errors.

Perelman But that has eluded us for years.

Boris Only because people have been looking in the wrong places.

Perelman Where is your family from, Boris?

Boris From Tomsk.

Perelman An unlikely place from which to contemplate the infinite. What does your father do?

Boris If you were kind you could call him an engineer.

Perelman And unkind?

Boris He works in construction.

Perelman Your mother?

Boris A nurse.

Perelman Do they tell you critical things? About our country? Or the system?

Boris On the contrary. My father is a committed Party member and patriot. He says to be born a Russian is to have won second prize in the lottery of life.

Perelman And the first?

Boris To have been born a Russian Jew.

Perelman is visibly touched.

Perelman Right, let's see how good you really are, Mr Berezovsky.

They begin their work.

SCENE FIVE

Litvinenko is with his ballroom-dancer wife, Marina. Standing in front of a large, expensive Mercedes.

Litvinenko Don't be so tense.

Marina I can't help it. I worry about damaging it, and the bills we'd have to pay.

Litvinenko He can afford the bills.

Marina And couldn't he have sent something other than a Maybach? It's so big. (*Walking round it.*) Why didn't he lend us one of his Ladas?

Litvinenko Because he has tens of thousands of those. Which means it doesn't feel special. He's trying to make an impression on you.

Marina On *you*.

Litvinenko No, on you. I told him you make the decisions in this family.

Marina But I'll be taking the test in a Lada.

Litvinenko Don't worry about the driving test. He's taken care of that. I have your new licence here.

Marina What?

Litvinenko With a letter from Boris to you.

Marina pulls over. Pulls the handbrake.

Marina Show it to me.

He does.

Not the licence, Sasha. The letter!

Litvinenko gives her the letter.

Look, handwritten. Surprisingly neat and elegant. He really took his time. And gave it thought. Read it to me!

Litvinenko opens it, and begins to read it aloud . . .

Litvinenko 'Dorogoia Marinochka, I have heard so much already about you from Sasha . . .'

Boris enters, and continues . . .

Boris '. . . during my failed attempts to persuade him to work for me. Perhaps you can help me in my campaign? I admire your husband very much indeed. He is brave and fearless and principled and that rarest of things, an honest cop trapped within a dishonest system. A patriot who looks around, and sees his beloved Russia falling apart. Like Sasha, I am also a patriot trying to wake up Russia after seventy years of slumber. I can introduce him to some of the most influential people in the country. To the President's closest circle, indeed to the President himself. For me it is just a phone call. In return I will have someone who will protect me, whatever it takes. This is not a "master–servant" arrangement: we are two fellow travellers. Two friends. Two brothers. And if, God willing, you succeed, perhaps one day you can then teach me ballroom dancing. I've always dreamt of being able to. Respectfully, Boris Berezovsky.'

Marina puts down the letter.

Marina Wow. I'm impressed. This is a man who sees and understands you, completely.

Litvinenko That's not enough reason to work for him. I joined the army aged seventeen and have given it my life.

Marina I know. But we can't make ends meet as it is. And you said the pay would be better?

Litvinenko It's not about the pay.

Marina Sasha, *five times* better. I've never tried to influence you in your career decisions. But I have noticed how unhappy you have become at work. And maybe his idea of Russia is better than the KGB's idea of Russia. It would certainly have more colour and music . . .

Over this: we fade in music.

SCENE SIX

Logovaz nightclub. Boris's office. Boris is reading, singing along to a song by his favourite singer, Vladimir Vysotsky.

Boris (*sings*)
'The bird-cherries are drying like a laundry in the wind
Yet the flowers of lilacs are falling like a rain,
Anyway I will take you from there
To the palace, where the flutes play
And you think that there's nothing more beautiful
    than that bewitched forest.'

Presently, he hears another voice. A man stands in the doorway in a cheap suit: Vladimir Putin.

Putin (*sings*)
'Let there be dew on the leaves in the morn
Let the moon be at loggerheads with the overcast skies,
Anyway I will take you from there
To the light tower-room with a view of the sea!'

Boris smiles. Putin smiles.

Boris Not many people know 'The Enchanted Forest'.

Putin I know all Vysotsky's songs.

Boris I sing them to myself. Mostly *in* enchanted forests while picking mushrooms. Where no one can hear. You?

Putin Me?

Boris You must sing to yourself, too.

Putin (*bashful*) I . . . I . . .

Boris Mmm? C'mon, Volodya. Where?

Putin (*shy, blushing*) Sometimes in the shower.

Boris In the shower!

Putin And driving my car.

Boris Driving your car! Do you still drive that piece-of-shit Zaporozhets? With 'sentimental value'.

Putin I do. But nowadays . . . as a taxi. You probably don't know, but I lost my job last month as Deputy Mayor.

Boris (*remembering*) Of course. The election. I'm sorry.

Putin The people that defeated us wanted me to stay on and work for them, but I couldn't do that. It would have devastated Sobchak.

Boris That's loyal.

Putin What is a man without loyalty?

Boris Rich, usually. So how can I help?

Putin I have come to ask a favour. But first let me say how sorry I am. What has a great country come to when people can attempt whack jobs and executions of one of our most prominent citizens in plain sight? I was horrified when I read it.

Boris One of the few advantages of surviving being blown up, and as a rule I wouldn't recommend it, is that you achieve a mythological status. The day I discharged myself from the hospital, I got a telephone call, summoning me to the Kremlin. Old Yeltsin himself wanted to see me! Of course, I went and expected him to express sympathy, maybe make some promises about cracking down on lawlessness, protecting Russia's most important business-men. Not a bit of it. He just wanted to stare and touch – my burns, my singed eyebrows, the gaps on my scalp where my hair had been. Then, of course, the jokes. Calling me 'Old Smokey', and 'Cinders', and 'Did anyone put the fire out?' The coarse laughter. The stench of vodka on everyone's breath. The big boys with big balls in the Kremlin. But then I looked at him, and I said, 'You may laugh, Mr President, but be careful when you make jokes about fate. It's clear my fate is to survive. What is yours?'

23

Putin You didn't say that?!

Boris I did! And silence descended in the room as they reappraise me – convinced that I must either have supernatural powers or that I've done some pact with the devil. And now Yeltsin can't get enough of me. Wants me around all the time. As a good-luck charm. A symbol of survival. And indestructibility.

Putin Actually, now you mention the President and your close association, it is for this reason that I came to see you. You might remember how I was able to help you sell your cars in St Petersburg.

Boris Of course.

Putin And you might also recall how, at the time, you wanted to compensate me in some way.

Boris I wanted to bribe you!

Putin And I refused.

Boris Because you're loyal! Now you're broke and you regret it! I understand, Volodya . . . How much?

Putin No, I don't want money. Before I was Deputy Mayor of St Petersburg, you may or may not know, I was in the Intelligence Services.

Boris (*freezes, takes a step back*) Oh.

Putin For sixteen years. It was a dream as a child. But these days politics interests me more.

Boris You no longer wish to police people, you wish to set them free?

Putin I am interested in liberalising Russia. We don't just need foreign investment to survive, we need foreign influence, and guidance and cooperation.

Boris Hear, hear.

Putin For too long we have defined ourselves as enemies of the West, we must become close to the West. Of course, that is the aim of the Yeltsin administration, and I have heard . . .

Boris notices his assistant in the doorway, meaningfully gesturing at his watch.

. . . they might be looking for people, cooperative people, like-minded people to help take this country in the right direction.

Boris Well, I would be happy to put in a word to Tatiana on your behalf.

Putin Tatiana *Yeltsin*? (*Star-struck.*) You would do that?

Boris Above almost all else, I pride myself on my judgement of character, and you, Volodya, are clearly a good man. It makes one wonder how you survived all those years in . . . where were you stationed?

Putin Dresden.

Boris Ahh. Well, that explains it. East Germany is where they generally sent the desk-jockeys, the altar boys, the softies, the 'B' team. Isn't that right? The alphas, the psychos, the real KGB men of action, got sent to London and Washington to do the proper work. (*Face falls.*) Oh, please, don't look so crushed. The fact you weren't speaks volumes in your favour. As a human being.

Putin (*eviscerated*) Thank you.

Boris I will speak to the Yeltsins and sing your praises and I'm sure they will do something for my friend from St Petersburg.

Putin I'm forever in your debt.

Boris Now, if you'll excuse me, there is a kid I cannot put off any longer.

The young businessman in his twenties, 'The Kid' (Roman Abramovich), enters.

Roman Abramovich. Vladimir Putin.

They look at one another. Two nobodies. A perfunctory handshake. Putin exits. Boris turns to Roman.

My God, they told me you were young. They didn't say you were an infant.

Roman Thank you for making time. And forgive me if I'm a little nervous.

Boris Why would you be nervous?

Roman To find myself face to face with you, finally! I'm a fan. Your biggest. Before anyone else you dared to make the move.

Boris I pounced!

Roman You understood . . .

Boris That the infinite was possible?

Roman . . . that the moment had come.

Boris 'Now or never.'

Roman When Gorbachev first permitted small-scale private enterprise you were in there . . .

Boris Like a shot . . .

Roman Borrowing Rubles from banks to pay manufacturers at the lower rate for export-class Ladas. But you made sure they never left the country. You then resold the cars back to Russians for three times the price, and delayed repayment to the banks until hyperinflation had rendered the original Ruble loans worthless!

Boris As they say, 'Time is money.'

Roman What I want to know is . . .

Boris How did I spend it?

Roman How did you know hyperinflation was just round the corner?

Boris When studying for my doctorate in applied mathematics, I spent years analysing how 'rational individuals behave under risk and uncertainty, and the decisions they make'. Which was fine, but hardly applicable to Russia during perestroika. When I saw society was unravelling I asked myself: 'What is the theory of how *ir*rational individuals might behave under risk and uncertainty?' The rest was paperwork.

Roman Truly it is an honour to meet with you. (*Hesitates, modest.*) I don't know if you know anything of me. I had my first success with a toy company. But now I've shifted my interests to oil. And last year alone I traded four point five million tonnes.

Boris So what is it you want from me? Your sorcerer's apprentice act is appealing but you seem to be doing just fine.

Roman I have been analysing my company. And have realised that, given the opportunity, it could do better, much better, if I were to vertically integrate.

Boris To create a single company.

Roman Yes, combine the production and refining business with my trading company. Which would overnight make it one of the world's largest single oil companies. But I'm no one, and have no influence with the government. What I need from you is to become a good family man.

Boris Of all the besotted Jewish mothers, mine ranks number one. But even she would not describe me as a good husband or father.

Roman Not that kind of family. The *family*.

Boris Oh. *That* family?

Roman I hear how enamoured the President and his daughter are of you. I hear talk of you being given a ministry position. You already own the State television station, which means you control public opinion, which makes you indispensable to the family. I need their permission to privatise. And expand into Europe where they are desperate for oil. And if I am associated with you . . .

Boris Ahhh. You want a Krysha.

Roman I do.

Boris A roof over your head. A bully on your side.

Roman *By* my side. A partner.

Boris How much profit does your trading company currently bring in?

Roman Forty million dollars a year.

Boris And if you were to pull this off . . .

Roman We.

Boris If *we* were to pull it off, to 'vertically integrate' oil and refinery companies, what kind of numbers would it generate?

Roman In year one? A hundred million. Conservatively.

Boris Please never be conservative around me.

Roman All right, with a favourable wind –

Boris Consider me a favourable hurricane.

Roman Three times that.

Boris And in five years?

Roman Three times that.

Boris stares. A long powerful silence.

Boris You understand that in return for my consultancy, my 'roof' . . . I would require certain funds.

Roman Of course.

Boris You also understand I never want to spell out what those funds might be for. I don't want to sign a contract, or even a deal. Nothing on paper. Nothing traceable. No 'definition'. But when you imagine a number, don't waste your time thinking about anything less than a fifty-per-cent share.

Roman stares.

You flinch, I can see that. But you don't refuse, which is smart. You have a conception of the infinite and you understand what it involves to get there. If I am to be your Krysha, your roof, your mentor and protector, I will ask a lot in return. You can have the very best of all worlds. But first you must make the right decision.

Roman stares at Boris. Then extends his hand.

Good decision.

They shake. Meaningfully. Fatefully.

You know, the West is shitting itself about the situation here in Russia. I have just returned from Davos where last week I had a two-hour private meeting with George Soros, who has heard unflattering stories of 'drunkenness', 'instability' and 'erratic' behaviour in the Kremlin. Of a lack of stability and authority. Of corruption and croneyism, of the potential collapse of the Ruble, and one of the most important economies of the world being destabilised absolutely. Like everyone else, Soros can see the Communists are enjoying a dangerous resurgence and are now openly considered the favourites to win the next election. He advised me that if I, a known associate of the Yeltsins, wanted to survive, and stay out of jail, I should leave the country immediately. 'What?' I said. 'Leave Russia? Never! I would sooner die!' And he said, 'Well, if you can't leave Russia, you have only one option.' 'What?' I said. 'To save Russia.'

As Boris speaks, several other suited men appear on stage. Boris widens his speech – from talking to Roman to talking to his fellow oligarchs:

And this, my friends, is why I have summoned you all here today. Because if the politicians cannot save Russia, then we businessmen must. I propose we put aside our differences, yes, even you and I, Gusinsky . . .

The others laugh.

. . . and work together to win this election for Yeltsin and make sure the Communists never get back into power. Between us, we have broadcast and print media covered. Petr and Mikhail, you have the monopoly on investment banking and telecommunications. Mikhail, you can provide the entire nation with oil and gas. With Anatoly managing the campaign we have all the tools we need for victory. We can do this. As oligarchs we can become modern Russian heroes.

The oligarchs work together – taking the 'puppet' Yeltsin and primping him, applying make-up. Removing his vodka. Using their television stations. Their newspapers. Their banks. Their vast resources. They are effectively taking over the 1996 election: pouring their money and resources into the campaign.

People already look at us in our limousines and our yachts and mansions, they see the way we live, and they dream to be us, the way our parents and grandparents dreamed to be the fathers of the revolution. They have seen us rescue precious State assets from the grasp of corrupt officials and turn them into gleaming enterprises. They hear us speak of a bright new future and it gives them hope. We cannot let them down. We must seize this moment to save the country we love. Lead the country we love. Free the country we love. And put the man that will make all that possible into the Kremlin. Okay?

Oligarchs Okay.

Boris Okay?

Oligarchs Okay!!

Boris has single-handedly turned things in Yeltsin's favour, and won their man the 1996 Presidential election. Boris and the oligarchs celebrate.

SCENE SEVEN

FSB Headquarters. Litvinenko enters. Inside: FSB heavies.

Litvinenko You asked to see me, Colonel?

FSB Boss Ah, Litvinenko.

An intimidating atmosphere of smoke, violence, decay, bullying and corruption. Litvinenko is not invited to sit.

Yes, I wanted to see you so that we may discuss the Jew Berezovsky. We understand he's offered you a job.

Litvinenko Which I declined because I already have a job.

FSB Boss Do you consider yourself a loyal servant of the Federation?

Litvinenko This is how I would describe myself before even I would describe myself as a husband and father.

FSB Boss Then I'm sure you'd agree, criminals cannot be allowed to interfere in the political process. Berezovsky and his businessmen friends are subverting the constitution and buying the election for their own interests. They need to be dealt with.

Litvinenko Can you be more specific, sir?

FSB Boss 'Dealt with'. So that he no longer causes problems for the State.

Litvinenko You have orders for this? Paperwork. From the directorate?

FSB Boss We don't need orders. We are an elite independent unit trusted to make our own decisions. And you, Lieutenant-Colonel, have in the past shown commendable 'willingness' and 'character' to go to the ultimate lengths to serve your country.

Litvinenko I'm sorry, are you really asking an officer to execute a fellow Russian . . . without a fair trial? Without justice? I think the Russian people would be interested to hear about this; the hit squads and corruption, the torture and racketeering.

FSB Boss That, Lieutenant-Colonel, would be a misjudgement.

Litvinenko No, the misjudgement was in you thinking I would go along with this madness. Twenty years I have been proud to wear the uniform, follow orders unquestioningly and risk my life. But I will not go along with it when the corruption and rot inside the system is worse than that which we are supposed to be fighting.

FSB Boss If I were you I'd think very carefully about what you are saying . . .

Litvinenko I have thought enough. As of today, I am no longer an officer of the FSB. (*Removes his ID, hands back badge.*) As of today, I work for Boris Berezovsky!

Litvinenko turns and faces an assembled press and TV conference.

Thank you for coming.

Flashbulbs, etc.

It saddens me to say the once great Federal Security Service of the Russian Federation is today corrupt and rotten absolutely and no better than a pigsty. Instead of its original constitutional aim of providing security for the State and citizens, it is now being used for settling scores and carrying out private, political and criminal orders for payment. Sometimes even for the purpose of political assassinations. I myself have resigned in disgust at what I have witnessed, and I hope and trust that with this – reluctant – public exposure, the once great FSB will find the courage to cleanse itself of the corruption and decadence that today fills its corridors, and return to its constitutional mission to keep Russia great.

Flashbulbs pop. A loud volley of questions for Litvinenko.

SCENE EIGHT

Logovaz nightclub. Boris is dining with Roman Abramovich.

Boris So imagine, we're in a café in Brussels, and the Vice-President of the IMF kicks off our conversation by telling me how concerned he is about the stability of the Ruble. I said, 'Then you and your international partners must prop it up, without delay.' 'Really? How much would it take?' he asks, cold fear in his eyes. Well . . . the speed at which we have reached this point has taken me somewhat by surprise, we have not even glanced at the menus, and the truth is I haven't the faintest fucking idea, so I look across the street, Rue de la Blah Blah, and see we are sitting opposite number forty-eight and I say, 'Four point eight billion!'

Roman (*laughing*) No!

Boris 'That is the number that will *temporarily* stabilise the Ruble and *temporarily* safeguard international markets.' Now the waiter has come. Standing there, waiting for our order. But no one is speaking and there is certainly no thought of food. 'All right,' he says. 'I will speak with my colleagues, but where would we pay it? We can't pay make a payment to your government – we hear terrible stories of corruption, and our information is that the Russian government could fall at any time and then our money would fall into the hands of the Communists!' I said, 'Personally, I would trust the government. But if you are uncomfortable with that . . .?' 'Please, Mr Berezovsky,' he says, 'tell us what to do. You're the only person we can trust.' I said, 'As it happens, I know a very trustworthy independent company that could act as intermediary to make sure the money ends up in the right hands.'

A secretary appears, holding a phone.

Secretary Vladimir Putin?

Boris What do you think? Shall we take it? Your call. Yes? No?

Roman Take it.

Boris Really? You're no fun. The man's only ringing to moan. Let's at least make him wait.

Boris counts to ten, looks at his watch. Roman gets the giggles, then, finally, Boris picks up the phone.

Well, well! If it isn't the new Director of the Federal Security Service.

Putin looks left and right. Lowers his voice.

Putin Not what I wanted, Boris. I wanted politics. I thought you had influence with Yeltsin.

Boris I do. And if I remember right, ten minutes ago you were a taxi driver. To me, this feels a lot better than a ride to the airport.

Putin That's not the point. The point is this is Intelligence.

Boris *Head* of Intelligence.

Putin Not what I was looking for.

Boris All right. I will go back, and put in another word with the family.

Putin As we agreed.

Boris As we agreed. But it's a pity, the FSB could use a good man, a principled man to lead them out of the darkness. And while we're on the subject of good, principled men, my friend and associate Alexander Litvinenko is just one such man. And he is being tortured and beaten in prison – for nothing.

Putin What Litvinenko did was not nothing – it was treachery – and I would advise you, in the strongest terms, to end your association with that man.

Boris Prison is for those that have broken the law. Litvinenko did not break any law. He's just . . . an 'enthusiast'.

Putin He held a press conference and publicly defamed the Secret Service. Defamation *is* a crime.

Boris He told journalists the truth; that his superior officer commissioned him to murder me.

Putin I can assure you an internal investigation was ordered. And the Colonel in question, a decorated hero of the Federation, denied all the charges.

Boris Of course! Because he doesn't want to end up in the salt mines where Litvinenko is now. Give him another chance, please?

Putin A traitor?

Boris Give him his freedom back and in return, I promise, I will speak to the family about getting you out of the Lubyanka building and into the Kremlin.

The Kremlin: a large, ornate chandelier. Boris is with Tatiana Yeltsin, daughter of the President.

Boris He was reasonable when he could have been difficult. Flexible when he could have been stubborn. And political enough to realise Litvinenko is not a hill to die on – nor worth making an enemy of . . . (*Indicating himself*.) . . . the most powerful man in Russia.

Tatiana The most powerful man in Russia is my father, the President. The second most powerful man in Russia is my husband because he's married to the President's daughter. The third most powerful person in Russia *might* just be you.

Boris Just meet him, Tanya. That's all I ask. You know how you've been looking for a replacement for Prime Minister Primakov. To find someone more 'supportive' of our interests.

Tatiana Which is why we decided Chernomyrdin.

Boris Chernomyrdin is yesterday's man.

Tatiana Or Silayev.

Boris The day before yesterday's man.

Tatiana Or Kiriyenko.

Boris Just another Primakov. I think this guy could be even better.

She looks at pictures of him.

Tatiana Vladimir Vladimirovich Putin? He's ex-Security Services. Those KGB guys, they're not like us. What rank did he reach?

Boris Lieutenant-Colonel.

Tatiana So he's a nobody?

Boris Precisely! A good thing! A 'nobody' is good at taking and following orders. Look at him, Tatiana. Side parting. Bless. Nice Western suits. Bless. Softly spoken. Bless. A child of poverty, brought up in a communal apartment. A good athlete, but not remarkable, a good student, but not remarkable, a good deputy mayor, liberal but not radical.

Tatiana He's a little . . . little.

Boris Nothing wrong with little!

Tatiana You're short, dear. Not little. He feels little. Little is dangerous. Little, in my experience, only ever wants to be perceived as big.

Boris In St Petersburg he did exactly what Sobchak told him to do. As Prime Minister he'll do exactly what *we* tell him to do. He's perfect. Happily married, with two daughters. Honest. Sober. Loyal. Who needs colour? Or personality? We just need a nice grey executioner of our wishes.

Tatiana Executor.

Boris What?

Tatiana I think you meant to say 'executor'.

SCENE TEN

BOOOM! An explosion.

Newscaster (*in Russian*) The bombs went off at three in the morning, killing innocent Russian families in the heart of Moscow. These cold-blooded attacks orchestrated by Chechen terrorists and aimed at the heart of the Russian capital . . .

Roman Abramovich enters.

Roman Am I too early?

Boris No, no! Come in! (*Indicates television.*) What do you think?

Vladimir Putin, the new Prime Minister, is giving a press conference on television.

Putin We will annihilate those responsible. We will track them down wherever they are and punish them severely. We will go not only after them but also after the people who shelter and encourage them. We shall destroy their planners and collaborators. I gave the order to the Security Services to act decisively and forcefully . . .

Roman Chechens. They will live to regret it.

Boris I don't mean the bombings. I mean our new Prime Minister. Who would have guessed? That he would have this much passion in him? This much fire?

Putin (*on TV*) Should there be even a hint of a threat to our security personnel, I gave them my permission to open fire to kill and not to take any prisoners. Liquidate the bandits on the spot. Scratch out the terrorists from their holes, hound them everywhere. At the airport, so be it at the airport. If, pardon me the expression, we catch them in the toilet, so we will finish them off when they are in shithouses. That's it – end of story. Nothing more to discuss!

Boris I will instruct them at the television station to play this footage round the clock. I will make sure the Russian people learn to love our little puppet.

He stares at the television.

Good, isn't it? (*With pride.*) The first high-definition television in Russia.

Roman Nice.

Boris Countless millions of pixels.

Roman And speaking of unaccountable millions . . . I asked for this meeting because I really would like some . . .

He is irritated by the sound of jazz piano playing . . .

I'm sorry. Would you mind asking him . . .? (*Indicates the piano music.*) It's ten in the morning.

Boris It's music! I like it. It soothes me. You were saying – you really would like . . .?

Roman Some definition.

He is still distracted/irritated by the music.

Boris About what? Define *yourself*.

Roman Our arrangement. Going forward.

Boris What about it?

Roman It's not quiiite how I imagined it.

Boris In which way?

Roman Well, the numbers for a start. 1996, thirty million. 1997, fifty. By 1998, eighty.

He turns, still irritated by the music.

And then the way payments are demanded. No invoices. No accountants. Just phone calls out of the blue, sometimes in the middle of the night. And it always has to be right away. Cash if possible. But sometimes paintings. Sometimes boats. It's . . . crazy.

Boris To be a Krysha is not an exact science.

Roman Well, I was hoping that things might become a little more specific, and precise. Like I said . . . I would appreciate a little more 'definition'. About where this is going and when it will end.

Boris Okay. Let me give you some 'definition'.

Boris spins round to the pianist.

SILENCE!! WHAT IS THIS IMBECILIC TINKERING?!
IT TORMENTS ME!!

*The piano immediately stops, terrified. Boris turns to
Roman. The mood changes.*

When you came to me you were a kid, a star-struck nobody,
with a pipe dream. Literally a dream about a pipe. And I
made it happen. Now you are a rich man, with a lot of
newfound power and newfound respect and if I were still
the same guy I was then, I might have to listen to you
as you come here, swinging your schmekel, asking for
'definition'. But a lot has changed for me, too. I am not just
a businessman with political connections. I now have an
actual position in government, in the State Duma, and not
just the ear but the gratitude of the drunken oaf President
whose re-election I secured. Furthermore, I can confirm
that said lame duck now wants to retire to alternately look
after the health of his heart and suckle on the tit of his
vodka bottle, and he comes to *me* to discuss who should
replace him. ME. ME!! That, in case you hadn't already
fathomed it, makes me something of a grey cardinal, a
kingmaker, and *you* still just a fucking businessman. So I
don't have to listen to you or your request for 'definition',
kiddo. If I want you to pay me money for services
rendered, you will pay me money, or paintings, or property,
or goats or boats or gold or silver or sheep or chickens and
in whatever denominations and whatever amounts I ask.
Okay?

Roman gets to his feet. 'Wow. That was excessive.'

Roman Okay.

Boris Okay?

Roman Yes, okay.

Boris Good.

SCENE ELEVEN

Moscow, 1989. Boris walks in. Professor Perelman works on a blackboard.

Boris *Shana Tova*, Professor.

Perelman turns, 'Sshh', and writes on a blackboard:

$$(1-1/s_1)\,(1-1/s_2)\ldots(1-1/s_n) = ?$$

Boris looks at it – shrugs, 'Simple', and writes:

$$51/2010\ldots(1-1/s_n)$$

Perelman I tease my poet friends sometimes, that the words they think are so precious – have no value at all. Two mathematicians, if accomplished enough, can have an entirely satisfying conversation in silence.

Boris But some things cannot be said in numbers.

Perelman Nothing worth hearing.

Boris Respected teacher. Respected friend.

Perelman Oh, dear.

Boris I came today to thank you for everything you have done for me. But the time has come for me to seize some of the opportunities, exciting opportunities, that are opening up all around us – and divert my energies elsewhere.

Perelman And abandon your work in mathematics and decision-making theory?

Boris Why as a rational man do you always reach for the most emotive word? I can never 'abandon' who or what I am. In my heart I will always be a mathematician, but in

41

the institute where I work there is no money for research. No money for salaries. No money for *food*. The system is broken. Russia is broken. And in this chaos, with the system collapsing, for the first time, Russian people find themselves with choices.

Perelman Theoretical choices.

Boris No, Professor, actual practical choices. We have always been taught there are no choices, no alternatives. No alternative forms of government, no alternative careers, no alternative schools, cars, televisions, homes. For more than half a century there was no need for a word in Russian for 'choice', since we had none. But that is changing, and having studied the underlying principles, having worked on the model, the equation that underpins the basis for all the errors, the suboptimal choices that people make that stop them being free, then perhaps I can save Russia from itself. We have only the finite to lose, but the infinite to gain! Imagine, in the West there is one car for every two adults. In Russia one car for every thousand.

Perelman In a world where people cannot afford to eat – who can afford cars? No, no. Stop, I beg you. You're right, the system is broken. The fall of Communism has left us all suffering not just a political but an ideological bereavement. Latvia, Lithuania, Estonia, Ukraine, Georgia, Moldova, have made sense of it as a liberation. But as Russians?

Boris We have been liberated too!

Perelman No, we haven't. We have been diminished. Humiliated. Stripped of our greatest asset, the Soviet Union, and in its place we have started going to church – joining hypnotic cults, fantasising about restoring monarchy – or embracing 'casino capitalism' in the hope it will make us feel whole again.

Boris It will.

Perelman Russia has spent so long as an empire it has no idea what she is as a country. A problem as complex as Russia is a conjecture that can never be solved. Even if it could – a simple solution – like 'bandit business' – is hardly the answer. Better to stay in here . . . (*Tapping head.*) The world of numbers where there are rules and order and regulation, and the State is always strong. Where all problems have a solution. And we are so close, within touching distance of a breakthrough. It would be a terrible mistake to abandon it now. Especially since I fear any deviation from academia will end in tears for you.

Boris And why is that?

Perelman This won't be easy for you to hear. It's your character. I worry you are constitutionally not suited to . . . freedom.

Boris Ha!

Perelman Based on my observation of you, your ambition . . . your desire always for the infinite. A personality like yours needs limitation and confinement. Here at the university you bounce around in safety. The ideas you consider exist only as ideas, or on paper. You in the real world? It scares me.

Boris Of course you are scared, you are too old to change. For all your talk of intellectual freedom, you cannot see how you have been imprisoned. Brainwashed! You are a product of the system. But for my generation a glorious wave has come. Washing away the authoritarianism, and the brutality. People don't want it any more. Russian people have had enough. They deserve better.

Perelman stares, dumbfounded.

Perelman I think I preferred it when we didn't talk. Let's go back to numbers. And *Shana Tova* to you.

43

The professor goes back to the blackboard and writes:

$$M = 2^{n-2} + 1 = ?$$

Boris replies in silence:

$$(1/s_2) \ldots (1-1/s_n) = 51/2010$$

Perelman writes again:

$$f(f(x)^2 y) = x^3 f(xy)$$

Perelman holds out his chalk to give to Boris. But Boris has gone.

SCENE TWELVE

Moscow, 1999. The face of Boris Yeltsin appears, on TV.

Yeltsin Happy New Year! Dear friends! My dear ones! Happy New Year!

A slurring, medicated Yeltsin addresses Russia on live television.

I am speaking to you for the last time as President of Russia. Today on the last day of the departing century I am resigning. I believed it would be easy to jump from the grey totalitarian Soviet past into a bright, rich and colourful future. But I was naive. The problems were too complex. So now it is time to hand over. Russia must enter the new millennium with new politicians, new faces, new hope.

Applauded by Boris and Tatiana. Putin walks on stage. The suit is more expensive, but he wears it tentatively.

A new President who can do more and do it better. In searching for the right man, I sought guidance from those closest to me, and on their recommendation have signed a decree entrusting the duties of the presidency to Prime

44

Minister Vladimir Vladimirovich Putin. Finally, let me just say to each of you: Be happy. You deserve happiness. You deserve happiness and peace. Happy New Year. Happy New Century, my people.

Boris and Tatiana clink champagne glasses, and go. Putin is left alone on stage. Unseen by him, a Chief of Staff figure enters. He clears his throat. Putin turns.

Voloshin Alexander Stalyevich Voloshin. Chief of the Presidential Administration. Is there anything I can do for you?

Putin No. Thank you. Everything's fine. Except . . . light switches?

Voloshin I know. The decorators hid them. Drives everyone mad. So . . . chandeliers, here. Table lights, here.

Putin And the . . .

Voloshin Bathroom? (*Indicates.*) That door. President Yeltsin found that it always needed two sharp pulls. Communist-era plumbing.

Putin Thank you. Why the banquet table?

Voloshin It's your desk, sir.

Putin Does it really need to be that big?

Voloshin It's the presidential desk.

Putin You don't think it will make me look little?

Voloshin I think it will make the person sitting opposite you look little.

Putin Right.

Voloshin You said there was something?

Putin Yes, I would like you to organise a meeting . . .

Voloshin Of course.

Putin With the following people: Anatoly Gref, Sergei Pugachov, Boris Nemtsov, Vladimir Potanin, Anatoly Chubais, Mikhail Fridman, Roman Abramovich, Mikhail Khodorkovsky, Eugene Shvidler, and your old friend . . . Boris Berezovsky.

Voloshin (*firm, definitive*) *Former* friend.

Putin They're busy people . . . they will all have complicated diaries, but as soon as possible.

Voloshin They really won't have complicated diaries. You're the *President*.

> *Voloshin goes. Putin is left alone in the presidential office. He looks at his surroundings.*

Putin So I am.

> *Blackout.*

ACT TWO

SCENE ONE

Putin is at his desk in the Kremlin. Boris storms in.

Boris Have you lost your fucking mind?

Putin I don't believe we have an appointment . . .

Two guards appear in the doorway. Look to Putin.

Boris In office barely five minutes and you've already developed a taste for grotesque symbolism?

Putin indicates the guards can go.

Late last night I get a call from Nemtsov who told me you summoned him, Potanin, Shvidler, Khodorkovsky, Chubais, Pugachov – and a dozen of Russia's most powerful businessmen to the outskirts of Moscow, to Stalin's dacha no less, kept them waiting an *hour*, then in you trot, or should I say, in trots nobody, literally a nobody, you sit at the head of some huge table, in Koba's favourite armchair and pronounce . . .

Putin 'Gentlemen, the party is over.'

Boris Gentlemen, the party is over.

Putin 'The State is the State.'

Boris The State is the fucking State!

Putin 'Business is business.'

Boris Business is fucking business!

Putin 'And politics is the business of the State.'

Boris You then went on . . .

47

Putin 'I understand that when Russia had an incapacitated, enfeebled President there was a power vacuum into which self-interested businessmen like you could step. Well, that vacuum no longer exists and as of today any businessmen who engage in political interference can expect to be prosecuted.'

Boris So, it's true?

Putin Yes. And I was surprised not to see you there. You were invited.

Boris I was busy.

Putin It's a foolish man that is too busy to meet his President.

Boris Not when he created that President.

Putin We might have to disagree about that.

Boris Not when he single-handedly plucked him from some provincial deputy mayor's cupboard, then placed him in the most powerful office in Russia.

Putin We might have to disagree about that, too.

Boris Fine, this is a game we can play. We can deny the floor beneath our feet and we can deny the ceiling above our heads, too. We can deny the sun and the moon and the tendency of day to follow night. It might pass the time and might even amuse us – but it won't get us very far. So why don't we just confine ourselves to the facts?

Putin The fact is I am President.

Boris And I put you there!!

Putin That's opinion. Not fact.

Boris I found you! FACT! Endorsed you! FACT! Sponsored you! FACT! Introduced you! FACT!

48

Created you! FACT, FACT, FACT!! You are my creation and now you presume to call meetings and call shots with my colleagues without my permission?

Putin The meeting was necessary to make clear the way things are going to be, the way things need to be if this country is to survive. A clear separation of business and politics.

Boris Oh, my God . . . (*Holding head.*) Only a former Head of the Security Services could be this naive! You cannot separate business and politics when the State is bankrupt. You need our money. Without the oligarchs you stand no chance.

Putin I see a country that has fallen into the hands of a handful of self-interested crooks. Priceless State assets have been snapped up by robbers, thieves . . .

Boris Assets which the State let fall apart and thanks to entrepreneurs are now functioning better than ever.

Putin And honest hard-working Russians are starving while a handful of 'kleptocrats' are not just rich, but obscenely rich. Richer than the State itself. It's wrong.

Boris Wrong/right/wrong/right.

Putin The State needs to reclaim its assets and its authority. A country cannot be run by businessmen. Social policy cannot be determined by businessmen! Foreign policy cannot be determined by businessmen!

Boris By whom, then? Politicians? Don't make me laugh. When was the last time you saw a politician you truly respect? Anywhere?! Never! Little people, grey people, mediocre people worming their way into office, then failing the minute they get there . . .

Putin And I say better a grey person who loves their country than a colourful one who loves only themselves.

Boris It's precisely because of my love of this country that I want to save it.

Putin By serving yourself first. By contrast I *have* served this country . . .

Boris As a low-ranking spook. A contemptible rat scurrying around the drainpipes of the Federation watching people, informing on people, sneaking on people. I am trying to save the country from creepy-crawly rodents like you.

Putin Then why did you put me here? As you keep claiming you did?

Boris To DO MY BIDDING!! To know your place and do the only thing you are capable of! The one thing sixteen years as a KGB jobsworth has prepared you for. To keep your nose down and follow orders!! Not have ideas above your station, not breathe rarified air and go mad! FOLLOW ORDERS like the appointee you are.

Putin Appointee?

Boris Yes. Appointee. Supplicant. Minion.

Putin Our time is over. 'Fact.'

Boris It's over when I say it's over. People like you don't 'dismiss' people like me.

    Putin presses a button on a desk. Three men appear
    in the doorway. It's suddenly a very intimidating
    atmosphere.

Bad decision.

    Boris storms out. As he leaves, we hear 'Time Forward'
    – the striking theme of Russia's nightly evening news.

SCENE TWO

*ORT television network (the all-powerful and influential
State television network watched by all Russia).*

Newscaster . . . reports are coming in of an incident in the
Barents Sea. The nuclear-powered Oscar II class submarine
Kursk was taking part in routine exercises when she
experienced minor technical difficulties. The vessel has
descended to the ocean floor – but authorities have
established contact with the crew – all of whom are alive
and well. Rescue efforts are currently under way. President
Putin has been notified of the incident and acted swiftly
and decisively to restore confidence . . .

Boris enters, agitated. Everyone gets to their feet.

Boris What is this crap?

Boris is given the script by a terrified journalist.

(*Reading.*) 'Minor technical difficulties'? There were two
huge explosions! 'Crew alive and well'? They're all fucking
dead! 'Rescue effort under way'? It's a farce! We can't even
find the submarine.

Boris pulls out a pen. As he starts making alterations –

When I took over this network, I made a pledge that the
truth which the people had long been deprived of would
finally be told. And what is the truth of this sad and sorry
episode? The crew never received adequate training,
lifeboats didn't work, torpedos were riddled with rust,
waiting to self-detonate, and our President did not act
'swiftly' or 'decisively'; he was water-skiing, on fucking
holiday, then too proud to engage with Western
governments who are trying to help. Meanwhile his sailors,
noble sons of Russia, suffocate and die needlessly on the
ocean floor? This is a national tragedy – another Chernobyl
– and we're singing the President's praises? I thought we
were interested in a modern democracy, freedom of speech?

51

Reporter We are.

Boris Then grow some balls and hold our leaders to account, finally. *This* is what I want you to say.

Boris hands over the script for the newscaster to speak.

Newscaster (*reading it, visibly pales*) I can't say that!

Boris Then you can clear your desk and get out. You're fired! Who will?

No hands. Finally, one terrified hand slowly goes up.

Good. See this person? He's our new anchor!

The music for the nightly news plays, the newly promoted newscaster takes his seat. We notice Putin has appeared on the side of the stage, and is watching the evening news. 'Three, two, one . . .'

Compromised Newscaster (*starting confidently*) Good evening. As Russia continues to grieve its dead sailors, more and more people are coming to the view that President Vladimir Putin has . . . (*Gulps.*) . . . criminally mishandled this national tragedy.

Boris Yes!

Compromised Newscaster His refusal to tell the world the truth or punish those responsible is . . . (*Clears throat.*) . . . an *insult* to the grieving families of the sailors . . .

Boris Boom!

Compromised Newscaster And a worrying return to Soviet-era lack of transparency and accountability.

Boris Get in!

Compromised Newscaster One has to ask if this former provincial deputy mayor is up to the job . . .

Boris Ha!

Compromised Newscaster (*dying inside*) Or perhaps he has simply spent too long in the Security Services – and no longer has a heart . . .

Boris And out the truth goes, beamed by transmitters, across eleven time zones and into every home across Russia . . .

Boris does a little victory jig of happiness. Putin's face, meanwhile, turns to stone. A silence, then:

Putin VOLOSHIN!

Chief of Staff Alexander Voloshin enters.

I want you to tell your 'friend' Boris Berezovsky that he will relinquish control of the national television station to me within two weeks. Failure to do so will result in prosecution.

Voloshin stares for an eternity. Then goes. Putin is left alone. He waits. Then looks in the mirror. And stares at himself. He looks right and left. Then regards himself. Not entirely sure of what he sees. He tries a few poses. As a thinker. As a leader. A strong man. Posing one way, then another. Wondering what fits best . . . Presently, Voloshin comes back. Putin snaps to a normal position. Tries to look normal.

And?

Voloshin I spoke to Berezovsky. And passed on your request.

Putin What did he say?

Voloshin 'No, thanks.'

Putin That doesn't sound like Boris.

Voloshin No. I . . . cleaned it up a bit.

Putin What were his actual words?

Voloshin 'Fuck off.'

Putin Right.

Voloshin And a few more besides.

Putin Go back and tell him if he does not relinquish control of the television station within forty-eight hours I will have him arrested on charges of tax evasion, illegal entrepreneurship and embezzlement of State funds. The State has a cudgel to use against people like Berezovsky. I have not used it yet; I am simply holding it in my hand. But if required, I assure you, I will use it. And will only need to use it once.

Voloshin Boss, are you sure? This guy is rich. And noisy. He has the wherewithal to set up a rival political party. Better someone like Berezovsky is inside the tent than outside. Hold your enemies close.

Putin And why would I do that, Alexander Stalyevich? 'Hold my enemies close'? When I can simply destroy them?

Voloshin stares, having never seen this side of Putin before. Then goes. Putin waits. Putin looks in the mirror again. That felt good. That felt really good. He feels taller now. He continues with his poses. A strong man. A tough man. A leader. Presently, Voloshin returns.

And? Did he come to his senses, or did he tell his President to 'fuck off' again?

Voloshin Neither. He's gone.

Putin turns.

Resigned his seat in the Duma and left the country.

SCENE THREE

South of France. Château de la Garoupe, Cap d'Antibes,
Côte d'Azur. Palm trees. Sunshine. Roman Abramovich is
being searched thoroughly by Litvinenko. And other
guards.

Roman How much security does a man need?

Boris You can accuse a man of paranoia after one
assassination attempt, but I think your new best friend
might want me dead, too.

Roman If you're talking about our President, he's not my
friend.

Boris Of course he's your friend. He just made you
Governor of Bumfuck Province.

Roman Chukotka.

Boris I thought there were supposed to be elections for
regional governors. But he's done away with them. Doesn't
that concern you?

Roman No friend would make one Governor of
Chukotka. It's a penance.

Boris What for?

Roman For being so loyal to you.

Boris Oh, please. It's a lover's gift. A heart-shaped
pendant. A bouquet.

Roman If you believe that, you fundamentally
misunderstand him, and me, and the balance of power
between us. And if you saw Chukotka – trust me –
(*Shudders to himself.*) you'd sooner be here in Antibes.
(*Looks around enviously.*) Is it the paradise it looks like?

Boris It was paradise when I could come and go. But even a French chateau loses its charm when you have to call it 'home'.

Roman Well, that's why I am here. To see if we can get you out of exile, back to your real home, and make you a rich man in the process.

Boris I am already a rich man.

Roman Then let me make you richer. Sell me your stake in ORT.

Boris Never.

Roman I've come with a hundred and fifty million dollars.

Boris We both know my stake is worth twice that.

Roman Don't make this difficult, please? I don't even want your share in a TV station. I have no interest in the media business. I'm just trying to mediate and make peace. For everyone. (*A beat.*) That was a serious miscalculation. To attack him like that.

Boris The miscalculation was *his*! To try to declare war on us oligarchs! The very people that got him in power!

Roman But what you did – the way you used your television station against him, to criticise him . . .

Boris Yes, criticise him!

Roman And humiliate him. Given the history between you, that was not just a 'response', it was a betrayal. A concept he cannot bear.

Boris I can think of a few more concepts he cannot bear. Freedom of speech. Justice. Law and order.

Roman Boris, please . . .

Boris I've started to look again into the Moscow apartment bombings by 'Chechen terrorists' that happened under his watch as Prime Minister. I used to think people were crazy when they said Putin himself was behind them, now I'm not so sure. False-flag terrorism. It's classic FSB and the perfect justification for his subsequent invasion of Chechnya. Making him look like a big 'Russian hero'.

Roman gets up. Walks away from their table.

Roman I came today to try and do you a favour. Because of the debt we acknowledge we *all* owe you. But I cannot listen to this.

Boris Because you don't want to admit the truth to yourself.

Roman Because it's . . . mad. Which makes me think it's time for us to reconsider our wider relationship, too.

Boris In which regard?

Roman Sibneft.

Boris You want me out of that, too?

Roman We've come up with a number. A very large number.

Boris Let me tell you something, kid, this is a moment far bigger than our 'business relationship'. This is a critical moment for all Russia. It's clear this man is not who we thought he was. If we don't act now, he will take us back to authoritarianism and brutality. Everything we have fought to change. We must intervene now before it's too late.

Roman And do what? Install a pro-Western government with Western-style democracy with Western values?

Boris Preferably.

Roman After what they just did to him? He does the unthinkable . . . he renounces two generations of Soviet orthodoxy, gets on his knees, and begs to join NATO. And instead of recognising the momentousness of the gesture, they tell him to get in line.

Boris Those are the rules of admission.

Roman Maybe, but Russia? Get in line? Please. This miracle is not going to happen overnight. Or move in straight lines. And people understand Russia needs a firm hand. They accept it. It's in their history and in their bones. A Federation that spans eleven time zones, fifty nationalities, one hundred and fifty million people, will change slowly.

Boris A wise professor once taught me that for every complex mathematical problem there was a simple solution that appeared to solve it, but that the simple solution was always wrong. Abandoning free speech and reform and liberalisation, and taking us back into the dark, is not the solution that a problem as complex as Russia requires.

Roman Well, before you cross the line beyond which it would be very difficult to return – I'd recommend you ask yourself one question. Is it possible you are dressing all this indignation up as 'patriotism', when maybe it isn't?

Boris What, then?

Roman Pride?

Boris Of course it's patriotism! You've seen what he's up to?

Roman It's also true that you gave the guy a leg-up, and you feel he never properly thanked you for it. Which leaves you with a decision to make. Either confront him and teach him a lesson . . . or accept where we are, be pragmatic and move on. He will get there. In time.

Boris Says who?

Roman Everyone who looks at it calmly. Rationally. And in the meantime there could be a good life for you, Boris.

Boris That would not be true to the man I now am.

Roman But it might be a good decision.

SCENE FOUR

A British Home Office spokesman walks on stage.

Home Office Spokesman The British Home Office has carefully considered the application submitted by Boris Berezovsky for political asylum in the United Kingdom, and is persuaded that his case has merit. His asylum is therefore granted as of September 9th, 2003.

We're in London. Boris and Litvinenko have assembled a group of journalists and give a large press conference.

Boris Thank you for coming. I am sure you have been following with interest the latest atrocities in Moscow. Suppression of the free and independent media. Political opponents being jailed without trial. All economic reforms stopped absolutely. Vladimir Putin is not interested in reforms, he is not interested in personal freedom. He is a nationalistic dictator interested in rebuilding a Russian superstate. We are here today to urge the West to open its eyes and see that this Russia will not be a good neighbour. It will threaten the world order, it will be an enemy of freedom, and we must act now.

Journalists are eagerly writing down these incendiary quotes.

There are three options for how to topple this extremely hostile regime. Option A I call the 'Palace Coup d'État' – started by people from the inner circle of Putin because even they must have realised by now what they are dealing with. Option B will be a revolution led by the Russian business elite. The third option, option C, is to topple Putin from *outside* Russia.

Boris and Litvinenko put on rubber 'Putin' masks. All the reporters laugh and take photos.

I call upon Western leaders to stop supporting Putin
because they continue to believe he is better than the
Communists – since in the long run his policies will never
be consistent with their interests.

*Flashlights pop. Journalists leave with great images
and great copy. Rrrringg: Boris's phone rings.*

Excuse me.

Boris, still wearing the mask, takes the phone call.

Hello?

At the other end, a familiar voice. Calling from Moscow.

Perelman Are you near a television?

Boris Professor Perelman!

Perelman Two American scientists, Daniel Kahneman and
Amos Tversky, have won the Nobel Prize for findings that
have revolutionised the study of decision-making theory.

*Boris removes the Putin mask as Kahneman speaks
to the world.*

Kahneman We know that decision-makers are not always
rational. What we didn't know was that these departures
from rationality can themselves be incorporated into
refined mathematical models . . .

Boris My Nobel Prize.

Perelman Yes. (*With disgust.*) Americans. (*He almost spits
the word.*) It should have been a Russian. It should have
been *you*. If you hadn't been . . .

Boris Too busy trying to save our country?

Perelman Too busy making bad decisions.

*Boris stares at the TV – wondering how it could all have
come to this. A man who realises he has lost everything.*

Kahneman I'd like to thank my mother, my agent, my friends and colleagues . . .

Boris exits the stage. Over this: the hypnotic throb and pulse sound of approaching helicopter rotor-blades . . .

SCENE FIVE

Chukotka. The most uninhabited region on earth. The sound of whistling wind. Otherwise total silence. And limitless, horizonless vastness and eternity.

Roman I brought you here, because it's where you get the best view.

Roman hands Putin a pair of large binoculars.

When we first started working together Boris used to talk to me about the 'infinite'. He said that as a non-mathematician I could never fully understand it. But it's *he* who has no idea. Because until you've been to Chukotka, you cannot pretend to comprehend limitlessness.

Putin stares at the vastness . . .

Putin How far are we from Moscow?

Roman Six thousand kilometres.

Putin It must have been lonely sometimes.

Roman It was. I made a habit of staying across the water in Alaska. People wrote about how as Governor of Chukotka I was opening up ties that had existed between the two regions for centuries. In fact it was just because Anchorage had the only decent hotel to stay.

Putin squints through his field glasses.

Putin Ah!

Roman See anything?

Putin Reindeer. Three, maybe four kilometres away.

Roman You can thank me for that. Things had got so bad here, food was so short, the people had no choice but to eat them. It was a fight for survival.

Putin And then you build schools, and hospitals, and create a programme of full employment – so now you're the saviour of the reindeer as well as the people?

Roman smiles.

It's been quite a success. Your governorship. Do you remember what you said when I first gave you the appointment?

Roman 'Why me?'

Putin (*mimics, whining*) 'Why me?'

Roman Of course. The only people one sends to the north-eastern wilderness are prisoners and enemies of the State. I thought it was a punishment.

Putin It was a test.

Roman Now I understand that.

Putin And what was the promise I gave?

Roman That it wouldn't be forever.

Putin It must have felt like forever sometimes. But you did it. You got out your chequebook, and did what I asked, without question. You understood loyalty matters. And thanks to your social responsibility and financial generosity I now look like a President who cares about the furthest reaches, the poorest people. The untouchables of the Federation. I will probably get credit for the reindeer too.

A silence. Putin lets it hang there.

Boris never understood that. That loyalty matters above all else, and that you can have all else as long as you are loyal. That's the only 'mathematical formula' he needs to understand. He also never understood that once a kingmaker has made a king he has created a problem for himself. He has created someone to whom he has to bow. So now he sits alone in London, plotting a 'new Russian Revolution' but all he really wants is to come home. He'd give all his money for me to make him Governor of Chukotka, because now he understands, surrounded as he is in 'metropolitan London' by his 'glittering British elite', *that* is the real wasteland with its hypocrisy and perfidy and snobbery. Here, with all its emptiness, it's still Russia. But he will never see Russia again. He crossed the line. Fifty million he sent to Ukraine, did you hear?

Roman No.

Putin To support an 'Orange Revolution' against his own country – the country he claims to love. Only Boris Berezovsky has the audacity to attack Russia with money he stole from Russia. So now round the clock we attack *him* on the TV station. The station he used to own. The station you bought back for me. (*Nods.*) Thank you for that, too.

Roman nods: 'Don't mention it.'

Boris was right about that. In the end I *do* need the oligarchs. Maybe that is what makes him most angry. To see how I agree with him, yet don't include him. I have chosen my oligarchs and he isn't one of them. What did you pay him in the end? To cut all ties?

Roman One point three billion.

Putin It should make him happy. In England, where they value money above everything, it makes him a star.

Roman But he hates England.

Putin Of course. And in Russia, one point three billion without a single friend in the Kremlin . . . (*Shrugs.*) . . . makes him . . . nobody.

The two men get back into the helicopter.

SCENE SIX

Boris's London Mayfair offices. Boris is busy and Litvinenko is irritating him.

Boris 'Scaramanga'?

Litvinenko '*Mella*'. Mario Scara*mella*. A former officer of the Italian Intelligence Services who came to me for the inside track on KGB and FSB activity in Italy as part of the Mitrokhin Commission . . .

Boris Sasha, is this important?

Litvinenko *Very*. I filled him in, so he owed me. Which is why, as soon as he got wind of this, Scaramella came to London to show me personally . . .

Boris Only I find myself in a little hot water with the British Home Secretary. I gave an interview to the *Guardian* newspaper last week and stated that since free speech and protest is now effectively outlawed in Russia, the only way to remove Vladimir Putin is through violence, but instead of inviting me to Number 10 Downing Street and asking my advice how to achieve that, Mr Quisling Jack Straw has written to me in person to tell me my asylum is unsafe. So much for our English friends.

Litvinenko shows him three crumpled, implausible-looking pieces of paper, email printouts.

Litvinenko A 'hit list' of enemies of the State of Russia. And guess who's number one? 'Russia's Osama bin Laden'?

64

Boris Who?

Litvinenko You!

Boris Me?

Litvinenko 'Boris Berezovsky', number one. With me number fourteen.

Boris I like being number one.

Litvinenko Have you heard of 'Dignity and Honour'? It's a group of fanatically loyal veteran Special Forces and FSB officers who make it their business to do the things they know the Kremlin would like but cannot be seen to do. Anyway, Scaramella tells me that specific assassins have been assigned to whack you and me . . . that we should increase our security and look out for someone with black hair with slim build, walking with a slight limp but an expert in judo with a good mastery of English and Portuguese.

Boris stares.

Boris Sasha. I'm busy. And you talk to me about spies and hit lists and Portuguese people with judo and limps. Go home.

Litvinenko You're not taking this seriously.

Boris No, I'm not. I love you, Sasha. From the day we met, in that God-awful hospital, I've considered us fellow travellers. More than that. Brothers. But you've been a little . . . intense recently. Relax.

Litvinenko I am going to meet someone else now, for tea. We can talk later.

Boris If you insist.

Litvinenko Oh, I almost forgot. (*Producing letter.*) An invitation from the leader of the Monarchist Party of Russia to meet for secret talks in Israel to discuss joining forces in opposition to Putin.

Boris Let me explain something. (*As if to a child.*) Here we have 'fringe'. Here we have 'lunatics'. And here . . . (*Gestures.*) . . . we have monarchists. Go home, Sasha? Please?

Rrriinggg! A lighting change. It's late at night. Boris's mobile phone rings.

Marina I don't want to disturb.

Boris checks a clock . . .

Boris Marinochka, it's late for you.

Marina You saw Sasha today, yes?

Boris Twice, yes.

Marina What time?

Boris First time around two? He was very agitated, you know how Sasha can be, but I was busy. Then he went to meet some people for tea, then around five or five thirty he came to my office again, but I was still busy, Zakayev was here and gave him a lift home.

Marina I just wanted to know if you ate something together.

Boris I had lunch in the office. Sasha had lunch with the Italian. Sushi, I think. Why?

Marina He's sick. Running to the bathroom all the time . . .

Boris Give him to me.

Marina He can't speak. It's quite bad.

Boris Then call a doctor.

Marina He won't let me. You know how he is.

Boris You have a spare room? Put him in there. These things generally last just a few hours. It will be better in the morning.

Rrriinggg! A lighting change. Boris's phone rings.

Boris (*woken from sleep*) Hello?

Marina It's no better, Boris. It's worse. He's in bed, screaming in pain. He keeps asking for the window to be opened.

We hear Litvinenko's screams of anguish and pain.

Boris Maybe he's hot?

Marina No, he's cold. Freezing cold. I've given him medicine to settle his stomach. But he can't keep anything down. I'm worried, Boris. You know how strong he is, he never complains. He's screaming all the time.

Rrriinggg! A lighting change. Boris's phone rings.

Last night he was unconscious, on life support. They told me I could go home, he would be stable. But after I left, his blood pressure fell suddenly. Catastrophically. And they could do nothing. (*A beat.*) He's gone, Boris. Gone.

Devastated, Boris hangs up. Then pulls out his mobile phone and starts dialling – deranged with anger. A lighting change. Putin appears on stage. His soft voice.

Putin I have nothing to say to you.

Boris 'Dissidents who have found legitimate sanctuary abroad enjoy immunity.' Those are the rules. What do you do? You send FSB fanatics with a bag full of radiation onto the streets of London.

Putin I have no idea what you are talking about.

Boris Alexander Litvinenko.

Putin Why would I have anything to do with that clown? The last I heard he was doing odd jobs in London.

Boris And, as it happens, running a revolutionary movement.

Putin Don't be absurd. Hanging out with no one. Speaking to no one. Of interest to no one. I have faith in the British police. With their pipes and their Dr Watsons. They will see this for what it is – one small-fry idiot who annoyed another small-fry idiot.

Boris Small-fry idiots don't have access to nuclear poison.

Putin Then maybe he upset someone slightly higher up.

Boris You, Vladimir Vladimirovich!

Putin No, not me. But maybe one of the many people who support me and can see the enormous challenges that I face and have grown tired of you and your associates. Tired of your treason and treachery, of your criminality and your disloyalty, of your perfidy and your whining and your obstructiveness and your thieving and plundering and your bribes and your decadence – all of which you dress up as patriotism and some kind of 'political movement' but is just you and your handyman, sorry, late handyman, jerking off into the void. You, Berezovsky, represent no one but yourself.

Boris Russia. I represent the Russian soul!

Putin Nothing! You represent *nothing* and speak for no one. You had your chance to be loyal to your President, and missed it. You had your chance to apologise, and squandered it. You lecture the world about decision-making and make one bad choice after another. Now, our two minutes are over.

Boris Wait! Hear me out.

Putin I granted this to you out of respect for the old times. I will never speak to you again.

> *Click: the line goes dead. A lighting change: we are in a press conference. Boris reaches into his pocket and produces a piece of paper.*

Boris I would like to read the final statement of Alexander Litvinenko.

Flashes from cameras.

(*Reading*) 'As I lie here . . . I can distinctly hear the beating of wings of the angel of death. I may be able to give him the slip . . . but I have to say my legs do not run as fast as I would like. This may then be the time to say one or two things to the person responsible for my condition. Vladimir Putin, you may succeed in silencing me but in doing so you have shown the world you are as barbaric and ruthless as your most hostile critics have claimed. You have shown you have no respect for life, liberty or any civilised value. You may succeed in silencing one man but the howl of protest from around the globe will echo in your ears for the rest of your life. May God forgive you for what you have done, but I'm confident the world has now seen what it needs to see and will take action.'

Boris folds up the letter. The media rush off and write their stories. Boris is left alone with Marina.

I give you my word I will not rest until I have avenged Sasha's murder and rid the country we all love of that monster. Putin was my mistake. Getting rid of him is my responsibility.

Marina Really, Boris? Is that wise? Isn't there a danger . . .

She hesitates, knowing this will not be easy to hear.

. . . that with someone like you, as controversial as you – that Putin becomes stronger by being seen in contrast to you? By being what Berezovksy is not? Does being the opposite of you – make him stronger? Maybe let others fight that fight.

Boris No, it's my fault – it falls to me.

Marina But how, Boris? In the past you had huge resources at your disposal. Money. A television station.

Boris I still have five point six billion dollars!

Marina No, you don't.

Boris On the contrary, I do. It's just sitting in the wrong person's bank account.

Marina Whose?

Boris The person whose Krysha I used to be. Who stole my money from me, when his 'new' Krysha told him to. But I will get it back, Marinochka. I will sue the Kid. Take him to court. And humiliate him. Break him. Reduce him to the wimpering little ingénue he was when I first met him. And then you and I will have the war chest we need to set up a rival political party to destroy . . . the other one. Him. Him. Him.

Marina Boris, stop all this. Be smart. You have children that barely know you. Find yourself a good woman, not always these young girls. Change your life. *Live* your life. You are lucky enough to still have one.

Marina goes, leaving Boris.

SCENE SEVEN

High Court, London.

Journalist Today, in a modest courtroom at the High Court in Fetter Lane, London, what's already being billed as 'The Trial of the Century' starts, as two billionaire Russian oligarchs, Boris Berezovsky and Roman Abramovich, former friends, now mortal enemies, face off in a fight to the death in the largest civil lawsuit in recorded history.

Boris takes the stand. All smiles and charm (almost flirtation) with the female judge . . .

Boris My lady, this is a story of two men. One senior, one junior; one mentor, one protégé; one master, one pupil; and how they worked together to acquire an asset – Sibneft – that would make them wealthy beyond their wildest dreams; until, that is, the senior, me, who had enjoyed a high political profile in Russia, and a great deal of influence, sadly fell out with those in power in the Kremlin and was forced to leave my home and create a new life abroad. This left the junior partner, Mr Abramovich, in a position where he was in effect required to make a choice: to remain loyal to his friend and mentor and the person to whom he entirely owed his great fortune, or instead, as we submit, to betray him and to seek to profit from his difficulties. I claim that I was cynically coerced into selling my fifty-per-cent stake by my protégé for the under-valued sum of one point three billion dollars. And that he – via his new close relationship with President Putin – threatened to make sure my interests in Sibneft would be expropriated by the Russian State if I did not sell.

Roman gets to his feet, and responds.

Roman My lady, the version we have just heard mixes fact and fiction in a way that reflects the extent of Mr Berezovsky's vanity and his self-deception. The fact is, Sibneft was my idea, my creation and my success.

Boris (*disbelieving*) What?!

Roman As to Mr Berezovsky having a fifty-per-cent stake? There are no legal documents anywhere that support this claim. While I accept Mr Berezovsky is the older, his seniority in age in no way reflects the seniority in our relationship. Mr Berezovsky was no more than my 'Krysha', an informal business arrangement or friendship that in no way relates to shareholdings.

Boris (*holding head*) No, stop, stop!

Roman The activities of a 'Krysha' might be hard for a person living in the United Kingdom today to understand.

And would certainly be hard for a court to establish legal precedence for. I'm told that in the British Isles one would have to go back to the fifteenth century to find anything remotely comparable . . .

Boris Excuse me? Am I hallucinating absolutely? Have I stepped through the looking-glass into a parallel universe? Are we gathered here today in Farringdon to rewrite Russian history? (*Gestures.*) E-ver-y-one knows that I am the owner of Sibneft. You don't need 'paperwork' or 'documentation'. Ask any toothless plasterer in Novosibirsk, or farmer in Yakutsk, or postman in Kurgan. They'll all tell you in their incomprehensible garlicky dialects. 'Sibneft? Boris Berezovsky!'

Judge Mr Berezovsky . . .!

Boris Lady Gloster, what is a courtroom if not a decision-making citadel? You have a very important decision to make today. This is not a battle for Sibneft, not even a battle for Russia, this is a battle for the whole free world.

Judge Enough! On my analysis of the evidence, I find Mr Berezovsky an unimpressive and inherently unreliable witness. At times the evidence he gave the court was deliberately dishonest, sometimes he was clearly making it up as he went along, and my ruling is that his case against the defendant has no merit whatsoever.

Over this: the sound of Vysotsky's guitar.

SCENE EIGHT

Boris is at home at his mansion in Surrey. He has sunk into a depression. He is with a young Russian woman.

Boris (*sings*)
'If a friend isn't a friend any more,
And he's neither a foe but a draw;

If you can't understand at once
If he's good – take a chance.
Take him once for a climb at dawn.'

Boris is listening to Vladimir Vysotsky singing 'Song about a Friend'.

Listen to this song . . . if you want advice for your life . . .
It's by Vladimir Vysotsky – you know him? You're too
young. But not too young to learn.

The music continues . . .

It's about who you can trust in life, and who you cannot . . .
he wrote it about four mountaineers . . . tied together with
ropes . . . attempting a dangerous and difficult summit . . .

The song, beloved by all Russians, is a hymn to friendship and betrayal – and Boris sings along.

Boris (*sings*)
'When your rope is the same as his
You will learn who he is.
If his spirit is lost at the start,
If he's scared when he steps on ice,
And when he slips then he cries.
Then you know that he may betray,
Do not chide him, just send him away:
Those, who are like him, don't belong,
They are not for a song.
If he did not repine, did not whine,
And when you fell from a cliff on ascent
He just groaned but held;
If he's been like a combat cohort,
On the peak has been high with your horde,
Then you know on bright day or dim . . .
YOU CAN COUNT ON HIM!'

Boris finishes with a flourish, lost in emotion. The song is full of meaning, pathos and significance for him. He turns to see how moved his companion is by all this . . .

But she has fallen asleep. Boris is left alone.
Alone in a mansion that isn't home, in the countryside
of a country for which he has no love, with a girl he
hardly knows, who would sooner sleep than listen to him.
Boris sits down, picks up a telephone. Dials a number.

Is it too early?

A lighting change: to reveal Professor Perelman in his
apartment in Moscow.

Perelman Of course, not. The early hours are always the best.

Boris Are you still in the same tiny Khruscheba apartment?

Perelman Yes.

Boris Scratching away at some conjecture or formula?

Perelman Yes.

Boris And perfectly content?

Perelman Of course. I have everything I need. Paper and pen.

Boris Did you ever find a woman?

Perelman I did!

Boris Professor Perelman! Good for you!

Perelman Three years after my mother passed, I finally ventured out. And on the third day, I found someone willing to give her life over to taking care of me.

Boris The third day?! How many women did you speak to before her?

Perelman None. She was the first.

Boris And you've been with her ever since?

Perelman Yes.

Boris Do you love her?

74

Perelman I do. That came after the seventh year. Quite suddenly, one day, it felt like my mother had never gone. Or maybe all the time I'd been with my mother, my feelings were just a precursor for Yulia. Which begs the question, did I love my mother as a woman or this woman as a mother?

Boris What conclusion did you reach?

Perelman That it doesn't matter.

Boris I don't think I've ever loved a woman. Or perhaps I've loved ten thousand women.

Perelman Please, don't exaggerate. You know how I insist on precision.

Boris I was being precise.

Perelman I tried to call you after the trial. I'm sorry. That was some humiliation.

Boris Was it on the news?

Perelman There was nothing *else* on the news.

Boris I used to *own* the news. (*Thinks.*) Is the music still Sviridov's 'Time Forward'?

Perelman Of course. Russia can survive countless political and economic revolutions. But she would never survive changing 'Time Forward' for the main evening news.

A silence.

Boris I miss our conversations. (*A beat.*) Actually, I miss everything. I realise I am in a twofold exile. From the country I love. And from myself. I despise being a businessman.

Perelman Then come back, Boris.

Boris He won't let me back.

Perelman He would if you came back as a mathematician.

Boris I'm not a mathematician any more.

Perelman Of course you are. We are all only ever who we were as children. Come back. I've something we could work on together. As a matter of fact, you could be its proof. (*Gestures.*) The limits of infinity.

Boris The point of infinity, as Archimedes proved, is it has no limits.

Perelman But you could prove its limitlessness *is* its limitation. In the end – there is no end. And without an end it has no definition. And without definition it amounts to nothing.

Boris Your problem, Professor, is you see confinement in infinity. And I see freedom.

Perelman Then explain something to me, Boris? How come it is you that is confined? While I am free?

SCENE NINE

The Kremlin. Putin welcomes Roman Abramovich back into his office.

Putin Welcome the TV star! All Russia has been glued to the nightly soap opera! Two great oligarchs in hand-to-hand combat. The Trial of the Century. Berezovsky – 'Booo!' – Abramovich – 'Hooray!'

Roman Stop, please.

Putin You know what my favourite moment was – apart from the verdict, of course? It was listening to a British court debating what is or what is not a 'Krysha'.

Roman Yes.

Putin Is it true, the rumour I heard? That Berezovsky called you?

Roman He asked to meet, last week. Face to face. I didn't feel there was anything left to say. But then he sent me this.

Roman reaches inside his jacket pocket and produces a sealed envelope.

And asked me to deliver it to you. Personally.

Roman hands it over. Putin perceptibly freezes. Cannot bring himself to touch it.

Putin Open it. Read it to me.

Roman No. My business with my former Krysha is done. Once and for all. This is your business with your former Krysha.

Putin Boris Berezovsky was never my Krysha.

Roman I at least acknowledge he made me rich. You won't acknowledge he made you President?

Roman goes. Putin calls after him.

Putin That was always his fantasy. His delusion. Another Boris made me President. Boris Yeltsin!

But Roman is gone. Putin is left alone with the letter. He stares at it on the table. As Putin stares . . .
A lighting change. And we see Boris composing the letter from his house in Sunninghill, in England. His prison. His exile.
In the Kremlin: Putin reaches out for the letter – and opens the envelope himself. He looks at the letter. Beautifully written. By hand. As he reads the letter . . .
In the UK: Boris speaks out the contents of the letter, as he reads it back to himself.

Boris 'My friend and President, my message comes in four parts. The first is an apology to you personally: for my arrogance and lack of respect. I used to ask myself when precisely it was that, thanks to me, you became your own man. The fact is, you were your own man long before I met you. The second is a request: to be able to return to the country that I love above all else, even money, even success. There are many things that separate us, Volodya, but the intensity of our patriotism is identical. The third is a pledge: to never re-engage in political activity of any kind and to show loyalty to *you* and to your administration. And the fourth is a commitment: to re-engage with the subject closest to my heart – mathematics – to live a quiet academic life and teach in the great universities. Grant me repatriation, and I will be forever your loyal and devoted servant.' (*Finishes writing, then, to himself.*) Supplicant. Minion.

Putin considers it all for a moment. Then presses a button. A secretary enters with a notepad.

Putin A letter. To Boris Berezovsky. (*Dictating.*) 'Your request to return to Russia to live a normal life while serious criminal charges remain against you is both unconstitutional and naive.'

The secretary writes.

'There is no room here for thieves or enemies of the State – sadly you have proven to be both. You say our patriotism is identical even if our politics is not. To me patriotism and politics cannot be separated. The Federation has enough world-class mathematicians and has no need for more. You have a new home now, in England. I urge you to try to enjoy it. But perhaps you have discovered already that no Russian can be happy living among his enemies. They are liars in the West, liars and hypocrites. Their food will never give you comfort, their humour will never make you laugh, and their women will never make you happy. Which is why you are so keen to come home. But your exile is an inevitable consequence of your actions. And exile is what you must suffer. This will be our last communication of any kind.'

His secretary finishes writing.

Secretary I will bring it back for review and signature.

She is about to go, then . . .

Putin (*calling her back*) Wait!

The secretary returns. Putin takes back the letter, looks at it, then tears it into tiny pieces.

He's not worth it.

Putin and his secretary go.

SCENE TEN

Boris is still alone – at his desk – in his vast mansion. Presently, his bodyguard, Avi, enters.

Boris Any reply? Any letters? From the Kremlin?

Avi No, boss. Nothing.

A silence. Boris visibly slumps.

Boris Leave me, will you?

Avi Boss?

Boris Go to the shops, Avi.

Avi What for?

Boris stares.

Boris You'll think of something.

Avi stares quizzically, then goes.
Left alone, Boris gets to his feet, takes off his silk scarf and tests its strength. He climbs onto a nearby chair, puts the scarf around his neck. Just then, a figure enters. Litvinenko's ghost. He enters, sees Boris on the chair.

Litvinenko (*rolls eyes*) Oh, for God's sake! What are you doing now?

Boris Am I being visited by ghosts now? I should have thought that was perfectly obvious.

Litvinenko Well, what good is that going to do?

Boris I've given up trying to do good.

Litvinenko I thought that was the point of Boris Berezovsky. He never gives up. At least leave some evidence of a break-in. Or a struggle. Leave an incriminating trail leading back to that bastard for people to discover. Like mine.

Boris You know, I never thought I'd envy anything about you – but I find myself envying your death.

Litvinenko It was fucking awful.

Boris But you were so brave. And there was such dignity in it. It was a magnificent, *political* death.

Litvinenko Thank you. In heaven, there are Russian dissidents that get to their feet when I walk into the room.

Boris You deserve it. You died for what you most passionately believed in life, and that's a gift not given to everyone. Sadly, my death will never be so heroic for one simple reason.

Litvinenko Which is?

Boris No one wants to kill me any more!

Litvinenko Don't be ridiculous. I know plenty of people who want you dead.

Boris Ex-wives?

Litvinenko Not just ex-wives! A whole host of people who really, really hate you!

Boris But not the one person that matters. He's happy for me to be alive. That's what's killing me. I am more useful to him alive than dead. My exile, my humiliations, my failure and isolation only serve to make him look good. Therefore I would sooner not exist – and leave only the absence of being. Like the number zero.

Litvinenko But the concept of zero does exist. In perfect spherical beauty. And has significance and power. As do you as a focal point for the opposition. An inspiration.

Boris There is no opposition. They're all gone. There is just him. And they love him.

Litvinenko They don't love him. When I was in prison there was one officer – he beat me brutally, like all the others – but I decided – maybe because he called me by my name, not a number – that there was compassion in him for me. And even though he broke my ribs, and shattered my nose, I told myself that he loved me. And so I loved him back. The Russian people love Putin like I loved that jailor.

Boris No. They *really* love him.

Boris hears the car approach.

That's my bodyguard returning. Go.

Litvinenko Are you sure?

Boris Yes. Take my mobile phone and leave it downstairs. They will never believe it was suicide if I was separated from my mobile phone.

Litvinenko can't help smiling.

Litvinenko I will, old friend.

Boris I was a patriot, you know. Above all else. Even mathematics. I want people to know that.

Litvinenko We were all patriots.

Litvinenko takes a last look at Boris, then arranges clothes on the floor, takes his mobile phone. Then goes. Boris is left alone. Over this:

Boris In the West you have no idea; you think of Russia as a cold, bleak place, full of hardship and cruelty. But ask any Russian to describe what would bring tears to their eyes if denied it – and they will tell you of singing songs by Vysotsky . . . picking mushrooms in the forests in summer . . . the sight of pelmenyi vendors in the streets. They will tell you of laughter in the banya with their closest friends every Saturday; the beauty of the snow on the rooftops – of eating ice-cream in the freezing cold. And of the comfort of being wrapped up against the wind in a shapka ushanka . . .

Boris hesitates for a moment, then jumps.

Blackout.

Patriots was first performed at the Almeida Theatre, London, on 2 July 2022. The cast, in alphabetical order, was as follows:

Assistant / Daniel Kahneman / Russian Captain
  Matt Concannon
Lawyer / Newscaster / Home Office Spokesman
  Stephen Fewell
Professor Perelman Ronald Guttman
Tatiana Yeltsin / Katya / Judge Aoife Hinds
Boris Berezovsky / Young Boris Tom Hollander
Vladimir Putin Will Keen
Marina Litvinenko / Nina Berezovsky Yolanda Kettle
Piotr / Alexander Voloshin Sean Kingsley
Alexander Korzhakov / FSB Boss / Avi / Boris Yeltsin
  Paul Kynman
Anna Berezovsky / Newscaster / Secretary Jessica Temple
Roman Abramovich Luke Thallon
Alexander Litvinenko Jamael Westman

Director Rupert Goold
Set Designer Miriam Buether
Co-Costume Designers Deborah Andrews
  and Miriam Buether
Lighting Designer Jack Knowles
Sound Designer and Composer Adam Cork
Casting Director Robert Sterne CDG
Voice Coach Joel Trill
Assistant Director Sophie Drake
Russia Consultant Yuri Goligorsky

Praise for *Patriots*:

'In this witty, thrilling battle of political wills, Peter Morgan . . . showcases the gift for concision and emotional grounding that [he] brought to *The Crown*, *The Queen*, and his New Labour succession drama *The Deal* . . . A cracking, exciting piece of theatre that's become, sadly, very timely.' *Evening Standard*

'The play is never less than gripping, delivered with crackling brio . . . a riveting, troubling piece.' *Financial Times*

'Lusciously livewire . . . This deliciously pell-mell hurtle through the years . . . zings with wit.' *Daily Telegraph*

'Gathering potency, gripping stillness and tension . . . *Patriots* looks to the past and traces a line not only around Berezovsky's rise, fall and final years of exile in Berkshire, but Putin's transformation from politician to autocrat . . . Fascinating.' *Guardian*

'Absorbing, acerbic . . . startlingly timely.' *Variety*

'Although written before Russia's invasion of Ukraine [in 2022], this political play by the writer of *The Crown* taps into current world events with masterful precision . . . There are the witty lines, the erudite speeches and the moral conundrums that we've come to expect from Morgan's work.' *Independent*